Wild Places
of the
Turks and Caicos Islands

Kim Mortimer

My obsession with photography has taken me on countless journeys to many wild places throughout the Turks and Caicos Islands. As much as this collection of images represents my love for photography and the awe inspiring country I am lucky enough to call home, it is also a map of my relationship with my husband. Every image captured was the result of years of exploration, logistical planning, camping and the many expeditions we've undertaken together. These pages would not have been achieved without him. I would also like to thank all the people who have assisted us in our adventures along the way. Please share with me the beauty and tranquillity that I have experienced while exploring these stunning islands.

Kim

KIM MORTIMER PUBLISHING

Providenciales
Turks and Caicos Islands

www.kimmortimerphotography.com

ISBN: 978-0-9934427-0-4

First Edition
Printed in South Korea

Front cover: Jerry Camp, South Caicos
Back cover: Beach, East Caicos
Title page: Sunset over Mudjin Harbour

The Turks and Caicos Islands are a wild and wonderful place to explore. The archipelago lies at the southern end of the Bahamas and consists almost entirely of limestone. The high porosity of the sediment means that there are no rivers and consequently very little soil runoff. The lack of nutrients in the warm tropical ocean also contributes to the striking clarity of the water. Coupled with the white sand and variable depths, the islands are blessed with some of the most dramatic and mesmerizing water colour on the planet.

Among the seven islands and forty plus cays of the Turks and Caicos are also found the most incredible beaches. The well-known beaches are impressive, but venture off the beaten path and you will find some true gems to call your own; at least for the day. The beaches are not the only appealing aspect of the coastline. A spectacular reef wall runs around the perimeter of the banks; a sheltered lagoon is created by the shallow barrier reef that runs offshore along the windward side of the islands; and the lee side is characterized by vibrant mangrove wetlands that provide a valuable habitat for bird and marine life. Together they are part of an integrated ecosystem that is as essential to the growth of the islands as it is to the life that it supports.

Venture inland through the coastal foliage and discover tropical dry forests, inland ponds and a veritable karst landscape that includes sinkholes, blue-holes and caves. For centuries the various environments have been used by the islands' diverse inhabitants to harness a living and some of their endeavours are briefly displayed in this book. Despite their shared history and the proximity of the islands to one another, each has its own unique allure that is definitely worth experiencing for yourself.

A sandbar south of Plandon Cay.

An idyllic day on the beach at Dickish Cay.

The clear turquoise waters of the Turks and Caicos Islands.

This tidal sandspit starts at Little Ambergris Cay and runs westward across the Caicos Banks.

Discarded conch shells surround a sandbar near Thatch Cay, East Caicos.

Named for a notorious seventeenth century pirate, French Cay is now a remote bird and wildlife sanctuary.

Breezy Point on the uninhabited island of East Caicos.

The old fisherman's hut at the northern point of Joe Grant's Cay boasts stunning views.

The Great House at Wade's Green Plantation on North Caicos.

An old plantation site located along the shores of remote Hog Cay.

When British Loyalists were expelled from the United States in the late eighteenth century, a number established cotton plantations in the Caicos Islands. Homes were built and walls were erected but the crop saw only short-lived success. A strong mortar was made by heating ground conch shells and limestone. It was used to good effect and helped preserve these practical structures for over 200 years.

One of the chimneys at Haulover Plantation on Middle Caicos.

A room with a view from Taylor's Hill on Salt Cay.

This old building on Big Ambergris Cay has become a haven for cacti.

Limestone walls can be found across the Turks and Caicos Islands.

Engravings made by sailors marooned on West Caicos in 1860.

An anchor encrusted in marine life lies in the shallows off Jacksonville.

An etching on the kitchen wall at Wade's Green Plantation.

Mudjin Harbour, Middle Caicos.

East Bay Cays National Park.

A sea cave along the windward coast of the Caicos Islands.

Drum Point, East Caicos.

This scenic mangrove channel snakes between McCartney Cay, Hog Cay and East Caicos.

Kayaking the stunning waters around the South Caicos peninsula.

Rocky Point, McCartney Cay.

Casuarina trees line a beach on McCartney Cay.

Exploring Little Ambergris Cay.

Goode Hill, East Caicos.

Cooling off in the sheltered waters between Joe Grant's Cay and East Caicos.

Sand ripples on a shallow sandbank off the coast of East Caicos.

A spectacular wall of stalactites reflects off the water in this subterranean room.

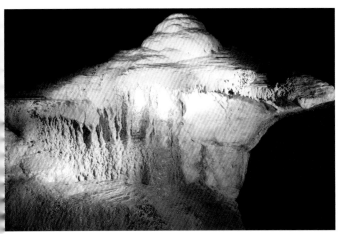

A dripping flowstone adorns a rocky podium.

Limestone caves, blue-holes and sinkholes are scattered throughout the many islands and often hidden deep in the undergrowth. They played a significant role in the lives of the Taino Indians and a few caves were later mined for the valuable bat guano that had accumulated inside. Some of the submerged systems have been found to host unique life forms including several minute endemic species.

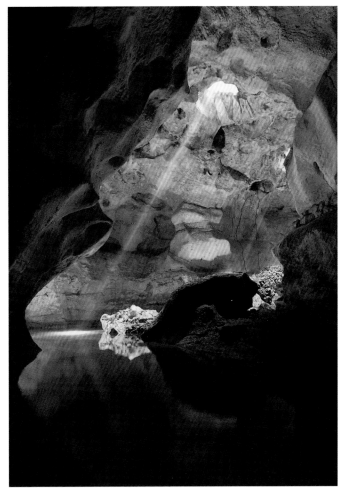

A beam of light hits the water in a hidden chamber.

Snorkelling through the mouth of Edison's Cathedral cave.

A lone root from a Strangler Fig tree descends through a skylight.

The extravagant but delicate cave formations in this wet cave can be thousands of years old.

Deep inside a cave system in the Caicos Islands.

Full column speleothems adorn a semi-submerged cave.

Small side tunnels branch off from the larger underground chambers.

A Taino Indian bowl preserved underwater

A Taino Indian petroglyph on a cave wall.

A Taino Indian fertility symbol.

Hiking the Crossing Place Trail on Middle Caicos.

The Fish Cays near the edge of the deep Columbus Passage provide a welcome anchorage when arriving from any direction.

Storm clouds build over Dove Cay and Long Cay in the Admiral Cockburn National Park.

One of the many beaches on Joe Grant's Cay which is sheltered by the offhsore barrier reef.

Wind driven pumps helped to manage the flow of water to different areas of the salt ponds like this relic in the Victoria Salina on South Caicos.

Stone walls separate the ponds on Salt Cay.

Salt production began during the seventeenth century when Bermudians sailed south to collect salt seasonally from the natural depressions in the low-lying Turks Islands. They later added stone infrastructure to formalize the ponds and also permanent residences which contributed to the charming architecture that is still evident on Grand Turk, Salt Cay and South Caicos. Salt was the mainstay of the Turks and Caicos Islands until all production ceased in the 1950s.

An old windmill pump on Salt Cay.

The Old Government House, Salt Cay.

Highland House, South Caicos.

The White House, Salt Cay.

Disused salt rakers huts on Salt Cay.

An old general store and home on South Caicos.

A residence on South Caicos.

A discarded organ sits outside a church on Salt Cay.

Garage, Salt Cay.

The causeway across Lake Catherine on West Caicos.

A large steam traction locomotive built by Charles Burrell & Co.

The island of West Caicos was briefly inhabited from the mid-nineteenth century. A causeway and narrow railway were built across the island to connect the salt ponds to a deep water harbour. In 1904 this 'iron giant' was mistakenly shipped from the UK to the island where it has stood still amongst the ruins of the Yankee Town settlement ever since.

Remnants of the railway tracks on West Caicos.

Big Sand Cay is a remote wildlife sanctuary in the southern Turks Islands.

This concrete bunker on top of Big Sand Cay held cables from an old US Naval listening post dating back to the Cold War.

The breath-taking leeward side of Big Sand Cay.

The beach forms a sandspit at its southern end.

A Brown Noddy nests on the isolated bird colony of Bush Cay.

A variety of animals inhabit the Turks and Caicos Islands both above and below the water. Ospreys, pelicans and wading birds are a familiar sight. Other marine birds roost and nest on the remote cays where Green and Hawksbill Turtles may also lay their eggs. Indigenous Rock Iguanas are common in low populated areas and even wild donkeys are prevalent on islands where they were once introduced.

Brown Noddies perch on the small island of French Cay.

Pink Flamingos are timid birds that frequent seasonal ponds in search of food and nesting areas like this one on Providenciales.

An Osprey nest on a rocky outcrop off Middle Caicos.

Reddish Egret hatchlings lie protected in a nest near Hog Cay.

Osprey eggs in a nest on White Cay overlooking Indian Cay.

Brown Pelican, Little Water Cay.

Yellow-crowned Night Heron, Big Ambergris Cay.

A Rainbow Boa-constrictor lies amongst the foliage on North Caicos.

A Rock Iguana marches across Half Moon Bay.

Nurse Sharks congregate during the summer mating season.

Wild donkeys roam South Caicos.

Iguanas and Turks Head cacti flourish on the uninhabited Fish Cays.

Turtle tracks are a welcome sight on remote cays.

Conch drying along the ridge of Bottle Creek on North Caicos.

Large piles of discarded conch shells on the edge of Plandon Cay.

These corrugated huts provide shelter for local fishermen on Plandon Cay.

Winter storms can create temporary lagoons like this one along the coast of Dickish Cay.

The north shore of Little Ambergris Cay.

A hidden beach in the Turks Islands.

Gibbs Cay is one of four islands in the Grand Turk Cays Land and Sea National Park.

There are many small cays scattered across the Turks and Caicos Islands. Some are easily explored while others are more isolated and best visited in fine weather. These windswept locations may appear to be desolate but many have amazing beaches and are a haven for well-adapted plant life, sea birds and reptiles.

Weather-beaten rocks in the Seal Cays Wildlife Sanctuary.

Pear Cay is one of a handful of small islands found in the remote Seal Cays Wildlife Sanctuary.

Natural arch on the windward side of the Turks Islands.

Dwarfed Joe Wood trees can live over 100 years.

Cacti cover many of the isolated cays.

Sea Purslane flourishes on the salty mudflats of Big Ambergris Cay.

The lush green interior of Bush Cay is a surprising find.

The Red Mangrove thrives in the tidal flats of Big Ambergris Cay.

Different mangrove species line this saltwater inlet on remote Bush Cay.

Sea oats prosper on the sand dunes of Gibbs Cay.

The scenic channel and low-lying cays near the old coastguard station on South Caicos.

A rocky point extends out into the turquoise waters of the southern Caicos Banks.

A remote beach in the southern Caicos Banks.

This beautiful entrance to the shallow wetlands inside Little Ambergris Cay becomes a bottleneck and makeshift hot spring on an outgoing tide.

The shifting sands of Little Ambergris Cay.

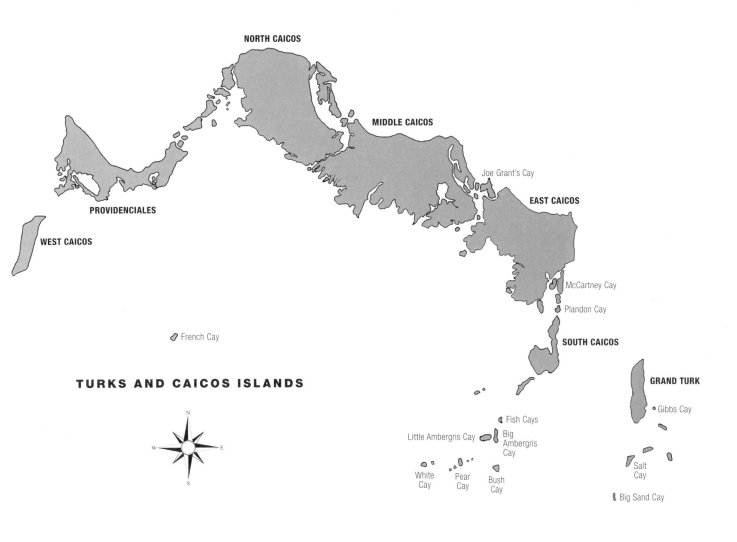

NORTH CAICOS

MIDDLE CAICOS

PROVIDENCIALES

Joe Grant's Cay

EAST CAICOS

WEST CAICOS

McCartney Cay

Plandon Cay

French Cay

SOUTH CAICOS

TURKS AND CAICOS ISLANDS

GRAND TURK

Gibbs Cay

Fish Cays

Little Ambergris Cay

Big Ambergris Cay

Salt Cay

White Cay

Pear Cay

Bush Cay

Big Sand Cay